TRAVELS TO THE WEST OF QIU CHANGCHUN

TRAVELS TO THE WEST OF QIU CHANGCHUN

As recorded by his disciple
LI CHI CH'ANG

TRANSLATED BY E. BRETSCHNEIDER (1888)

WWW.BIGFONBOOKS.COM

ISBN: 978-1-957990-44-6

Contents

Introduction

K'iu Ch'ang Ch'un was an eminent Taoist monk born in 1148 CE and thus elderly at the time of his trip. He was ordered by Chingis Khan to travel to his court, which at the time encamped in Central Asia. The route went through the Altai and Tienshan mountains, the southern parts of today's Kazakhstan, through Kyrgyzstan, to Samarkand and then down into NE Iran and Afghanistan. He was accompanied by his disciple Li Chi ch'ang who composed the narrative—a rather detailed diary of the journey. It was published with an introduction by Sun si in 1228 and included in the Tao tsang tsi yao.

Bretschneider observes that this account "occupies a higher place than many reports of our European mediaeval tavellers." It is indeed a brilliant account of Central Asia at the time, providing insight into many areas including geography, the life of ordinary people, Mongol administration, travel conditions, and even a more endearing and benevolent portrait of emperor Chinghis himself.

The text has been excerpted from E. Bretschneider's Mediæval Researches from Eastern Asiatic Sources (New York: Barnes & Noble, 1888), pp.37-108. Bretschneider's page numbers are included here in the format .

Chinghis Khan's letter of invitation to Ch'ang ch'un

Heaven has abandoned China owing to its haughtiness and extravagant luxury. But I, living in the northern wilderness, have not inordinate passions. I hate luxury and exercise moderation. I have only one coat and one food. I eat the same food and am dressed in the same tatters as my humble herdsmen. I consider the people my children, and take an interest in talented men as if they were my brothers. We always agree in our principles, and we are always united by mutual affection. At military exercises I am always in the front, and in time of battle am never behind. In the space of seven years I have succeeded in accomplishing a great work, and uniting the whole world in one empire. I have not myself distinguished qualities.

But the government of the Kin is inconstant, and therefore Heaven assists me to obtain the throne (of the Kin). The Sung to the south, the Hui ho to the north, the Hia to the east, and the barbarians in the west, all together have acknowledged my supremacy. It seems to me that since the remote time of our shan yü such a vast empire has not been seen. But as my calling is high, the obligations incumbent on me are also heavy; and I fear that in my ruling there may be something wanting. To cross a river we make boats and rudders. Likewise we invite sage men, and choose out assistants for keeping the empire in good order. Since the time I came to the throne I have always taken to heart the ruling of my people; but I could not find worthy men to occupy the places of the three (kung) and the nine (k'ing). With respect to these circumstances I inquired, and heard that thou, master, hast penetrated the truth, and that thou walkest in the path of right. Deeply learned and much experienced, thou hast much explored the laws. Thy sanctity is become manifest. Thou hast conserved the rigorous rules of the ancient sages. Thou art endowed with the eminent talents of celebrated men. For a long time thou hast lived in the caverns of the rocks, and hast retired from the world; but to thee the people who have acquired sanctity repair, like clouds on the path of the immortals, in innumerable multitudes. I knew that after the war thou hadst continued to live in Shan tung, at the same place, and I was always thinking of thee. I know the stories of the returning from the river Wei in the same cart, and of the invitations in the reed hut three times repeated. But what shall I do?

We are separated by mountains and plains of great extent, and I cannot meet thee. I can only descend from the throne and stand by the side. I have fasted and washed . I have ordered my adjutant, Liu Chung lu, to prepare an escort and a cart for thee. Do not be afraid of the thousand li. I implore thee to move thy sainted steps. Do not think of the extent of the sandy desert. Commiserate the people in the present situation of affairs, or have pity upon me, and communicate to me the means of preserving life. I shall serve thee myself. I hope that at least thou wilt leave me a trifle of thy wisdom. Say only one word to me and I shall be happy. In this letter I have briefly expressed my thoughts, and hope that thou wilt understand them. I hope also that thou, having penetrated the principles of the great tao, sympathisest with all that is right, and wilt not resist the wishes of the people.

May 15,1219

[Chang ch'un's answer to Chinghiz:]

K'iu Ch'u ki [Ch'ang chun], from Si hia hien, devoted to the tao, received lately from afar the most high decree. I must observe that all the people near the sea-shore are without talent. I confess that in worldly matters I am dull, and have not succeeded in investigating the tao, although I tried hard in every possible way. I have grown old and am not yet dead. My repute has spread over all kingdoms; but as to my sanctity, I am not better than ordinary people, and when I look inwards, I am deeply ashamed of myself. Who knows my hidden thoughts? Before this I have had several invitations from the southern capital and from the Sung, and have not gone. But now, at the first call of the Dragon court (he means the Mongol court), I am ready. Why? I have heard that the emperor has been gifted by Heaven with such valour and wisdom as has never been seen in ancient times or in our own days. Majestic splendour is accompanied by justice. The Chinese people as well as the barbarians have acknowledged the emperor's supremacy. At first I was undecided whether I would hide myself in the mountains or flee (to an island) into the sea, but I dared not oppose the order. I decided to brave frost and snow in order to be once presented to the emperor. I heard at first that your Majesty's chariot was not farther than north of Huan chou and Fu chou. But after arriving at Yen (Peking), I was informed that it had moved far away, it was not known how many thousand li. Storm and dust never cease obscuring the heavens. I am old and infirm, and fear that I shall be unable to endure the pains of such a long journey, and that perhaps I cannot reach your majesty; and even should I reach, I would not be good for anything. Public affairs and affairs of war are not within my capacity. The doctrine of the tao teaches to restrain the passions; but that is a very difficult task. Considering these reasons, I conferred with Liu Chung lu, and asked him that I might wait in Yen or in Te hing (now Pao an chou) the return of your majesty. But he would not agree to that, and thus I myself undertook to lay my case before the emperor. I am anxious to satisfy the desire of your majesty, and to brave frost and snow, wherefore I solicit the decision (whether I shall start or wait). We were four who at the same time became ordained monks. Three have attained sanctity. Only I have undeservedly the repute of a sainted man. My appearance is parched, my body is weak. I am waiting for your majesty's order.

April of 1220

(Sun Si, in his preface to the narrative, says)

Ch'ang ch'un was a man of a high perfection. At the time I attained the age of manhood (I had heard much of him, but) I conceived that this venerable man must long ago have soared up to heaven, and after his transformation lived in the company of the clouds in the high spheres of the universe, and was sorry at not having seen him. But in the winter of the year 1219 there was suddenly a rumour that the master, who lived near the sea (in Shan tung), was invited (by Chinghiz) to set out on a journey. In the next year, in spring (1220), he arrived indeed at Yen king (Peking), and stayed in the monastery of Yü su kuan. Then I had the satisfaction of seeing, him personally.

When he sat, his position was immovable, like a dead body; when he stood upright, he resembled a tree ; his movements were like the thunder, and he walked like the wind. From his conversation I learned that he was a man who had seen and heard much. There was no book which he had not read. From day to day I felt an increasing veneration for him. The number of men, attracted by his glory, who solicited the favour of being his disciples, increased every day. When the express (despatched by Chinghiz) arrived for the second time, the master set out for the west.

At his departure his disciples asked him

when he would return. He said, "After three years." This happened in the first month of 1221, and indeed, in the first month of 1224, the master returned from the west after just three years' absence, as he predicted. The master, in his journey to the west, travelled over more than 20,000 li. He saw places which are not laid down on our maps, and which are not moistened by rain or dew. Although he was received everywhere with great honours, the journey was very painful for him. Nevertheless he was always cheerful, liked conversation, and wrote verses. He loved nature in her various aspects. At every place he stopped at, he visited all that was remarkable. As regards his views of life and death, he considered them like warmth and cold, but thoughts about them did not perplex his mind. Could he enjoy such perfections if not penetrated by the tao (true doctrine)?

July 2nd 1228

In the year 1220, the emperor Che'ng-gi-sz' (Chinghiz) sent his adjutant Liu Chung lu, with an escort of twenty Mongols, to Ch'ang ch'un, who then was in Shan tune. Liu Chung lu transmitted to him an invitation from the emperor and a golden tablet, on which an order was written to treat the master in the way the emperor himself was wont to be treated. Chung lu reported that in the fifth month (May, June) of 1219 he received from the emperor the order to seek the master. The emperor at that time was in the wu-li-do of the Nai-niang Ch'ang ch'un agreed to go with Chung lu, and chose nineteen from among his disciples to accompany him. In the beginning (February) of 1220 they set out for the north, and arrived at Yen (Peking) towards the end of the second month (beginning of April), where the master was received with great homage.

In Yen the master was informed that Chinghiz had moved to the west, and he felt apprehensive that his advanced age would not permit of his enduring the fatigue of a long journey. He wished to await the time of Chinghiz' return in order to be presented, and it was resolved to ask the permission of the emperor. There was yet another question which alarmed Ch'ang ch'un. Chung lu, by order of his sovereign, had assembled a number of girls to be brought to the emperor's harem. The master said, "Owing to actresses having been sent from the kingdom of Tsi to the kingdom of Lu, Confucius left Lu (which was his native country). Although I am only a savage of the mountains," how can I travel in the company of girls?" In order to lay before the emperor these questions, Chung lu despatched a courier with a report, and the master sent also an address to the emperor.

On the 15th of the fourth month (May 18) 1220, the master with his disciples and Liu kung left Yen (Peking), and travelled to the north. The way led through Ku yung. One night, at the northern exit (of the pass), we met a gang of robbers; but they bowed and said, "We do not harm the master."

In the fifth month (June) we arrived at Te hing, and passed the summer there in the temple of Lung yang kuan.

At the beginning of the winter (1220) A-li-sien arrived, sent by the prince O-ch'en, and soon after another envoy came. They invited the master to call upon the prince on his way to the emperor. He made an affirmative sign with his head. In the same month, the courier sent to Chinghiz returned, and brought a letter from the emperor to the master, in which the latter was again invited in the most flattering terms. Chung lu also received a letter, with the imperial order to take the greatest care of the sage. The master then conferring with Chung lu said: "Now the winter is beginning, the way through the desert is cold and distant; our companions have not purchased all things required for such a long journey. Would it not be better to pass the winter in Luug yang kuan, and start in spring?" Chung lu agreed, and so they passed the winter there.

On the 8th of the first month (February 1), 1221, we started again. It was a fine day; the friends of the master brought presents, and standing before his horse, shed tears, and asked hüi: "Master, you undertake a distant journey of several tens of thousands of li; when shall we have the happiness of again bowing before you?" The master replied: "If you will be strong in the faith, I shall meet you again." As the friends pressed the question, he said evasively: "Our staying and our travelling depend not on our own will." But the friends would not desist, and wished a decisive answer. Then the master said: "I will be back in three years--in three years." He repeated it twice.

On the 10th of the first month (February 3, 1221) we passed the night at Ts'ui ping k'ou. The next day we passed the defile called Ye-hu ling. To the south we saw the T'ai hang ling and other mountains. The mountain air was delicious. Towards the north there were only cold sandy deserts and parched grass. Here are the limits of the breath of Chinese nature. We saw a field of battle covered with bleached human bones.

Travelling farther to the north, we passed Fu chou; and on the 15th (February 8), proceeding in a north-eastern direction, arrived at a salt lake called Kai-li po. Here we saw the first settlements- about twenty houses. To the south was a salt lake with many sinuosities, which stretched to the north-east. From this (northward) no rivers are met, water being obtained only by wells dug in the sand. Neither are there any considerable mountains for several thousand li farther to the north. After five days' travelling on horseback we left the boundary-line called Ming ch'ang.

In six or seven days we arrived at a great sandy desert, to Sha t'o. In low places elm trees of a dwarf size are found. Some of them are of a considerable circumference ;11$ but from this in a north-eastern direction extending more than ten thousand li, no tree is to be seen. We left the sandy desert on the 1st of the third mouth (March 25, 1221), and arrived at a place called Yü-rh-li, where we began to find settlements. The people for the greater part are engaged in agriculture and fishing.

At that time it was tsing ming) (fifteen days after the spring equinox), but there was no trace of spring, and the ice was not yet melted.

On the 5th of the third month (March 29) we started again, and travelled in a north-eastern direction. All around we saw habitations, consisting of black carts and white tents. The people here are nomads, and change their abode according to the prevalence of water and pasture. No tree could be seen, and we met only yellow clouds (of dust) and decayed grass.

Finally, after twenty days and more without changing the direction, we reached a sandy river, which flows to the north-west, and discharges itself into the Lu kü river.

We crossed the sandy river, the water coming up to the girths of the horses. The borders of the river were overgrown with willow-trees. After travelling three days in a northern direction, we entered the siào Sha t'o (little Sha t'o desert).

On the 1st of the fourth month (April 23), 1221, we reached the encampment of the prince O-ch'en At that time the ice was only beginning to melt, and the first green was seen on the ground. There was a wedding being celebrated, and many Mongol chiefs had arrived with mare's milk. We saw several thousands of black carts and felt tents standing in long rows. On the 7th (April 29) the master was presented to the prince, who asked him about the means of prolonging life. As it would have been unbecoming that the prince should hear the precepts of the master before the master had seen the emperor, it was agreed that on his return the master should call again on the prince. On the 17th the prince ordered that a hundred horses and bullocks should be given to expedite the master, and we started again (May 9).

Our way led in a north-western direction. On the 22nd of the fourth month (May 14) we reached the river Lu-kü (or Kerulun), which here forms a lake of several hundreds of li in circumference. When the waves rise by the wind, great fish are thrown out, and the Mongols catch them easily. We then went along the southern shore of the river (Kerulun). We found abundance of ye hie everywhere. On the 1st of the fifth month (May 23), at noon, an eclipse of the sun happened, while we were on the southern bank of the river. It was so dark that the stars could be seen, but soon it brightened up again. In this country it is cold in the morning but warm in the evening. We saw huang hua (yellow flowers) in abundance. The river flows to the north-east. On both banks of it are many high willow trees, which the Mongols use for making their tents.

After a journey of sixteen days (up the Kerulun, along its southern bank), we arrived at the place where the river changes its direction, winding round the hills to the north-west. We could ascertain nothing about its sources. Farther to the south-west we reached the post- road, which leads to Yü rh li. The Mongols here were very glad to see the master. They brought him millet, and said that they had been waiting for him for a year. The master made them a present of jujubes. They had never before seen this fruit.

From this we travelled ten days. At the time of the summer solstice the shadow (of the gnomon) measured three feet six or seven inches.

Here we noticed the peaks of high mountains; the country we traversed westward was throughout mountainous or hilly.

The population was numerous, all living in black carts and white tents. The people are engaged in breeding cattle and hunting. They dress in furs and skins, and live upon milk and flesh-meat.

The men and unmarried young women plait their hair so that it hangs down over their ears. The married women put on their heads a thing made of the bark of trees, two feet high, which they sometimes cover with woollen cloth, or, as the rich used to do, with red silk stuff. This cap is provided with a long tail, which they call yu-yu, and which resembles a goose or duck. They are always in fear that somebody might inadvertently run against this cap. Therefore, when entering a tent, they are accustomed to go backward, inclining their heads.

These people (the Mongols) have no writing. They settle their matters by verbal convention, and when they enter into contracts they cut certain marks on wood. They are never- disobedient to orders, and never break their word. They have preserved the customs of the early ages.

Farther on, after four stations, to the north-west we crossed a river beyond which a plain extended with luxurious grass and abounding in water. The plain was surrounded by mountains with picturesque valleys. On the east and on the west (of the river?) we saw the ruins of an ancient city. We could recognise the position of the streets. There is a tradition that this city was built by the K'i-tan. We found, indeed, on the soil a tile with letters of the K'i-tan. This was probably a city founded by those K'i-tan warriors who emigrated, unwilling to submit to the new dynasty. We were told, also, that the city of Sün-sz'-kan (Samarkand) lay more than 10,000 li to the southwest, that it was built on the best place in the country of the Hui-ho (Mohammedans), and that it was the capital of the K'i-tan dynasty, of which seven emperors had reigned there.

On the 13th of the sixth month (July 3), 1221, we passed over a mountain called Ch'ang sung ling (mountain of high pines), and stopped on the other side. There were so many pines and kuai trees. They grow so high as to reach the clouds, and so dense that the sunbeams cannot penetrate them. They predominate in the valleys on the northern slope of the mountain. On the southern slope few are found.

On the 14th (July 4) we passed over a mountain, crossed a shallow river, and passed the night in a plain. It was frightfully cold, and the next morning we found a thin coat of ice on the water. The natives said that generally in the fifth or sixth month snow begins to fall in this country, and that, happily, this year it was not so cold as in other years; therefore the master changed the name of the mountain into Ta hag ling (mountain of the great cold). Rain here is always accompanied by hail.

Thence we went more than a hundred li to the southwest, through a mountainous country, on a winding road. There was a stony river, more than fifty li long, the banks of which were about a hundred feet high. The water in the river was clear and cold, and bubbled like sonorous jade. On the steep bank we saw a large kind of onion, three or four feet high. In the valleys splendid pine trees were growing, of more than a hundred feet in height. The mountains stretched to the west in a continuous chain, all covered with tall pine trees. We were five or six days travelling in these mountains, the road winding round the peaks. It was magnificent scenery, the slopes of the rocks covered with noble forests, with the river gliding through the depths below. On level places pines and birches were growing together. Then we ascended a high mountain which resembled a large rainbow, overlooking an abyss of several thousand feet deep. It was dreadful to look down to the lake in the depth.

On the 28th of the sixth month (July 18) we stopped to the east of the wu-li-do (ordo) of the empress. Chung lu (the adjutant) sent an express to announce our arrival, and the empress immediately sent an invitation to the master. We crossed a shallow river which flows to the north-east, the water of which came only up to the axle of the cart, and then entered the encampment. On the southern bank of the river there were more than a thousand carts and tents.

The Chinese princess and the princess of

Hia both sent presents of millet and silver.

At this place eighty kin of flour cost fifty liang; for the flour is brought from beyond the Yin shan, a distance of more than 2000 li, on camels, by the Western barbarians. Although it was the hot season we had no flies in our tents. Wu-li-do (in Mongol) means in Chinese hing kung. Carts and tents had all a magnificent appearance, such as was unknown to the ancient Shan yu.

On the 9th of the seventh month (July 29), 1221, we left the Ordo, and travelled in a south-western direction five or six days. Several times we saw snow on the tops of the mountains, and at their base we often met with grave-mounds. On the top of one of the mountains we found traces of sacrifices offered to the spirits (of the mountains). After two or three days we passed over a mountain which rises in the form of a pointed peak. It was covered with pines and kuai trees. To the west was a lake. We passed through a vast defile to the south, and found a river flowing westward. On the northern side we saw a great variety of trees, and for more than twenty li we found on our road abundance of kiu and fragrant grass. To the north lay ruins of an ancient city, Ho-la-siao.

Proceeding to the south-west, we passed about twenty li through a sandy desert, where water and grass were scarce. There we saw the first Hui-ho, who were occupied irrigating their fields by means of aqueducts. After five or six days' travelling we reached a mountain, and having passed on its southern side, rested at a Mongol encampment (station), passing the night in a tent. At daybreak we started again, and travelled along the Nan shan (southern mountains), on which we saw snow. The master wrote a poem (detailing his journey from Fu chou to the mountains mentioned). At the station we were told that to the north of these snowy mountains is T'ien Chen-hai ba-la-ho-sun. Ba-la-ha-sun (balgassun) is the same as "city" in Chinese. There are magazines of corn; therefore the city is also called ts'ang t'au (the head of magazines).

On the 25th of the seventh month (August 14) a number of Chinamen, artisans and workmen, who lived there, came in procession to see the master. They were all ravished; met him with exclamations of joy, bowed before him, and accompanied him with variegated umbrellas and fragrant flowers. There were also two concubines of the Kin emperor, Chang tsung, and the mother of a Chinese princess, who met the master with exclamations and tears. The latter said: "For a long time I have heard of your reputation and your virtues, and was always grieved at not having seen you; but now, unexpectedly, I have met you in this country."

The next day Chen-hai arrived from the northern side of the A-bu-han mountain. Ch ang ch'un said to him that he was much surprised at seeing the people ruled by Chen-hai carrying on agriculture, for in the desert this is a rarity. He also asked Chen-hai's opinion about the question of remaining there and waiting the return of the emperor. Chen-hai declared that he lately had received orders from Chinghiz to expedite the master when he arrived in this country, as soon as possible, and that he would be responsible for the master's staying there for any length of time. He manifested his intention to go with the master, so that the latter could not object, and decided to proceed on his journey again. Chen-hai observed further, that in the regions they would have to pass through now there were precipitous mountains and large marshes which could not be traversed by carts. He proposed to travel on horseback, and to restrict the number of the suite and the carts. The master agreed, and left nine of his disciples behind. A monastery was built for them, in the construction of which everybody assisted--the rich with money and the workmen with their labour; so that in less than a month the edifice was finished. It was named Si hia kuan (Si hia was the name of Ch'ang ch'un's native place).

On the 8th of the eighth month (August 26), 1221, the master started again, taking with him ten disciples. There were only two carts with the caravan, and more than twenty Mongols from the station (encampment) accompanied him. Liu kung and Chen-hai had also a hundred riders with them. The way led to the west, in the vicinity of high mountains. One of the servants of Chen-hai reported that these mountains had a bad fame for their goblins, and that once a goblin pulled him by the hair. Chen-hai narrated further, that once it occurred also to the Khan of the Naiman, who passed through this country, to be charmed by a goblin, and that he was obliged to offer a sacrifice to him. The master did not make any remark on these tales.

After having travelled south-westward about three days, we turned to the south-east, passed a great mountain, proceeded through a vast defile, and on the 15th of the eighth month (September 2) we were at the north-eastern side of the Kin shan mountains (the Altai). We stopped here for some time, and then went south. These mountains are very high and vast, with deep defiles and long slopes. There is no road for carts. The road over these mountains was planned and constructed by the third prince, at the time the army went to the west. The hundred riders (who formed the escort) were ordered, at difficult ascents, to pull our carts by ropes, and to place drags upon the wheels when descending. In the space of about three stations (three days' journey) we crossed successively three ridges of mountains, and arrived then at the southern side of the mountain (they had now crossed the Kin shan), where we stopped near a river, at a place abounding in water and grass.

Here tents were pitched, and we were waiting several days for bullocks and horses. The master (profiting from this rest) made three poems (in which he celebrates the scenery of the Kin shan).

After having crossed the river, we proceeded southward and passed over a low mountain with stones of different colours. On the sides of this mountain no tree or grass was found. Within seventy li we saw two red-coloured hills; and thirty li farther, stopped at a fresh-water well in the midst of a salt desert, where we prepared our food with this water. The grass around the well was much trampled down by sheep and horses.

Chung lu then had a conference with Chen-hai about our journey. He said: "We are come now to the most difficult part of the road; what is your opinion?" Chenhai replied: "I have known these places well for a long time;" and addressing the master he said: "We have before us the po ku t'ien (field of white bones). It is thickly strewn all over with black stones. We have to travel more than 200 li to reach the northern border of the Sha t'o (sandy desert), where we shall find plenty of water and grass; then we have to cross the great Sha t'o, in extent about 100 li (from north to south). This desert extends west and east, I cannot tell exactly how many thousand li. On the other (southern) side of the desert is a town of the Hui-ho. There only shall we find water and grass again." The master asked: " What do you mean by 'field of white bones'?" Chen-hai replied: "That is an old battlefield--a field of death. At one time a whole army perished there by exhaustion; no one escaped. A short time ago, at the same place, the army of the Naiman was destroyed. Whoever crosses the desert in the daytime and in clear weather (i.e., exposed to the sun) will die from fatigue, and his horse also. Only when starting in the evening, and travelling the whole night, is it possible to reach water and grass on the next day by noon."

After a short rest we started in the afternoon. On our road we saw more than a hundred large sand-hills, which seemed to swim like big ships in the midst of the waves. The next day, between eight and ten o'clock in the morning, we reached a town. We did not get tired travelling at night- time, only we were afraid of being charmed by goblins in the darkness. To prevent charms, we rubbed the heads of our horses with blood. When the master saw this operation he smiled and said: "Goblins flee away when they meet a good man; as it is written in the books. It does not suit a Taoist to entertain such thoughts."

At sunset we started again, leaving behind on the road all our tired-out bullocks, and put six horses to every cart; henceforth we used no more bullocks.

At the time we were still at the northern border of the great desert, we had observed on the southern horizon something like a silver-hued morning twilight. We asked our companions, but nobody knew what it was. Then the master said: "That must be the Yin shah mountain chain." The next day, after crossing the desert, we met some woodcutters, and asked them. They confirmed the words of the master. It was the Yin shan.

On the 27th of the eighth month (September 14), 1221, we arrived at the northern side of the Yin shan. There was a small town (the town of the Hui-ho, spoken of by Chen-hai). The Hui-ho came to meet the master, and the chief of the town presented fruits and Persian linen cloth (Po-sz' pu). He told us that 300 li distant, on the other side of the Yin shan, there was the city of Huo chow; that it was very hot there, and that Huo chou was celebrated for the abundance of grapes.

The next day we proceeded westward along a river, and passed two small towns. At this time (middle of September) wheat was just beginning to get ripe. The land was artificially irrigated by spring-water (conducted from the mountains), for rain is rare there.

Travelling farther to the west, we reached a large city called Bie-sz'-ma. The wang (ruler or prince), the officers, the people, the Buddhist and Taoist priests, &c., came long distances out of the city to meet the master. We lodged in a vineyard west of the city. The relatives of the wang of the Hui-ho brought wine made of grapes, various fruits, &c. The devotion the people felt for the master increased from day to day. In his company were seen Buddhists, Taoists, and Confucionists. The master inquired much about the country and its customs. They told us that at the time of the Tang dynasty (618-907) this city was the tuan fu of Pei t'ing, and that up to this time the frontier towns established by the Tang still exist. They related further, that several hundred li to the east is a fu (city of a department) called Si liang, and 300 li to the west a hien (district city) called Lun t'ai.

The master asked what they reckoned the distance to the place where the emperor (Chinghiz) then was. All agreed in estimating it at 10,000 li and more to the south-west.

On the 2d of the ninth month (September 19) we started again, and after four days' journey westward, stopped east of the city of Lun t'ai, where the chief of the Tie-sie came to meet us.

To the south, on the Yin shan mountains, we saw three rugged peaks supporting the heavens. The master dedicated a long poem to them.

After having passed two towns, we arrived on the 9th of the ninth month (September 26) at a city of the Hui-ho called Ch'ang-ba-la. The wang (ruler, prince) there was a Wei-wu-rh. He was an old friend of Chen hai, and came with his relatives and priests of the Hui-ho to meet us far outside of the city. After our arrival there, he presented us a dinner on a terrace, and his wife regaled us with wine. They brought also very heavy watermelons and sweet melons.

The master received the visit of a Buddhist priest, and spoke with him by means of an interpreter. It must be observed that the country from this place eastward belonged to China at the time of the Tang dynasty. West of it there are neither Buddhists nor Taoists. The Hui-ho [Muslims] only worship the west.

The next day we proceeded farther to the west, and went along (the northern slope of) the Yin shan as far as about ten stations. We crossed also a sandy desert, where the loose sand is collected by the wind into moving hillocks, resembling the waves of the sea. No vegetation is visible there; the carts cut deeply into the sand, and the horses also sink. To cross this sandy desert took a whole day's journey. This is probably a part of the great desert (which Chen-hai) called the field of white bones. It is bounded to the south by the Yin shan mountains.

After leaving the sandy desert, we travelled five days, and stopped on the northern side of the Yin shan. The next day, early in the morning, we proceeded southward on a long slope seventy or eighty li, and stopped in the evening to rest. The air was cold; we found no water. The next day we started again, and travelled southwest-ward, and at a distance of twenty li suddenly got sight of a splendid lake of about 200 li in circumference, enclosed on all sides by snow-topped peaks, which were reflected in the water. The master named it the Lake of Heaven.

Following the shore, we descended in a southern direction, and on either side saw nothing but perpendicular cliffs and rugged peaks. The mountains were covered to their summits with dense forests, consisting, of birches and pine trees more than a hundred feet high. The river winds through the gorge for about sixty or seventy li, with a rapid current, sometimes shooting down in cascades. The second prince, who was with the emperor at the time he went to the west (in 1219), first made a way through these mountains, cut through the rocks, and built forty-eight bridges with the wood cut on the mountains. The bridges are so wide that two carts can pass side by side.

We passed the night in the defile, and left the next morning; then entered a broad valley which stretched from east to west, well watered, with abundant grass, and here and there some mulberry trees or jujubes.

The next station from this was the city of A-li-ma, which was reached on the 27th of the ninth month (October 14). The ruler of the realm of Pu-su-man came out of the city, together with the Mongol ta-lu-huachi [governor], to meet the master. We stopped at a fruit orchard west (of the city). The people here call a fruit a-li-ma; and as the place is famed for its fruits, the city received the above name. There is a kind of cloth called the tu-lu-ma. The people say that it is woven from vegetable wool. We got seven pieces of it for winter clothes. This hair resembles the down (enclosing the seeds) of our willows. It is very clean, fine, and soft; and they use it for making thread, ropes, cloth, and wadding. In cultivating the fields, the people use also artificial irrigation by means of aqueducts. For drawing water they use a jar, which they bear on their heads. When they saw our Chinese pail for drawing water, they were much delighted, and said: " You T'ao-hua-shi are very able men." They call the Chinese T'ao-hua-shi.

Journeying farther westward, we arrived in four days at the T'a-la-su mo-lien. The river, which is deep and broad, comes from the east, and cutting across the Yin shan mountains, runs in a north-western direction. To the south of the river, again, are snow- covered mountains. On the 1st of the tenth month (October 17) we crossed the river in a boat, and proceeding southward, arrived at a great mountain, on the northern side of which was a small town. Thence we travelled five days to the west. As the master travelled by imperial order, and as we now approached the encampment of Chinghiz, Chung lu went in advance to announce to the emperor the arrival of the sage, while Chen-hai remained with the latter.

Travelling again westward during seven days, we crossed a mountain, and met a Chinese envoy, who was returning to China. The envoy bowed before the tent of the master, who asked him: "When did you leave?" The envoy answered: "I saw Chinghiz for the last time on the 12th of the seventh month (1st of August). The emperor is pursuing the Suan- tuan Han [sultan of Khorezm] to Yin-du (India)."

Next day there was a great snowfall, and we reached a small town of the Hui-ho (Mohammedans). The snow was one foot deep, but was quickly melted by the sun.

On the 16th of the tenth month (November 1), 1221, we went in a south-western direction, crossed a river on a bridge of planks, and in the evening reached the foot of the southern mountains. Here were (formerly) the dominions of Ta shi Lin-ya, who was a descendant of the Liao. As the armies of the Kin subdued the Liao, Ta shi Lin-ya with several thousand men withdrew to the north-west. After ten years' peregrination from one place to another, he finally reached this country.

Here the climate is quite different from that of the regions north of the Yin shan (T'ien shan). The country has many plains, and the people are employed in agriculture and breeding of silkworms. They make wine from grapes. The fruits there are about the same as in China. It does not rain there during the whole summer and autumn; hence the fields are irrigated artificially by canals led off from the rivers, and the corn is brought to maturity. To the north-east are mountains; to the southwest low countries, which stretch out for ten thousand li. This kingdom (of the Karakhitai) existed about a hundred years. As the power of the Naiman was broken, they fled (i.e., Guchluk, the son of Tayank Khan, chief of this tribe) to the Ta shi Lin-ya, and after becoming powerful, overthrew that nation (the Karakhitai). Subsequently the suan-tuan (Sultan of Khorezm) conquered the western part of their dominions. Then Chinghiz arrived; the Nai man (Guchluk) were totally destroyed, and the suan-tuan was also overthrown.

We were informed that the way still before us presented many difficulties. One of our carts was broken, and, we were obliged to leave it behind.

On the 18th of the tenth month (November 3) we travelled westward along the mountains. After seven or eight days' journey, the mountains suddenly turned to the south. We saw a city built of red stones, and there were the traces of an ancient military encampment. To the west we saw great grave-mounds, which resembled the tou sing (the constellation of Ursa major). Passing over a stone bridge, and travelling five days along the south-western mountains, we arrived at the city of Sai-lan. There is a small tower in Sai-lan. The ruler, a Mohammedan, came to meet us, and directed us to our lodging. During the first days of the eleventh month much rain fell.

The 4th of the eleventh month (November 20), 1221, was the new year of the country-people. They were walking in parties congratulating each other.

On the same day Chao Kiu ku (one of Ch'ang ch'un's disciples) said to one of his companions: "At the time I resolved, in Süan te, to follow the master, I felt the omen of the long journey (i.e., he had a presentiment that he was leaving never to return), and during my journey my heart has always been sad. But I followed the precepts of our master, who teaches that thoughts about dying and living ought not to perplex the mind of a man of the true doctrine (Taoist). His heart ought not to be excited by thoughts about joy and sorrow. Whatever, too, may happen in life is good. I feel that now the term of my returning (i.e., of his death) is near. You, friends, serve faithfully our father." After a short sickness of several days, he died on the 5th of the eleventh month.

Thence we proceeded south-westward, and arrived after three days at a city, the ruler of which, likewise a Mohammedan, met and regaled us. The next day we passed another city, and after two days' travelling reached the river Ho-Wan mu-lien. We crossed it on a floating bridge, and stopped on its western bank. The guardian of the bridge presented to Chen- hai a fish with an enormous mouth and without scales. The sources of this river are in the south-east, between two snowy mountains; its water is muddy and runs rapidly, the depth being several chang [10 Chinese feet]. It flows to the north-west, it is unknown how many thousand li, being bounded on the south-west by a desert, without water or grass, extending more than 200 li; for which reason we travelled there in the night. We went southward to high mountains covered with snow (in winter), and then to the west. These mountains are connected with the southern mountains of Sie-mi-sz'-kan (Samarkand).

We then arrived at a city where we found grass and water, and farther on passed another city, the chief of which, a Mohammedan, came to meet us, and entertained us at a place south of the city with a dinner and wine. By his orders boys performed some plays, dancing with swords and climbing on poles. After this we passed two cities more, travelled half a day among mountains, and came out at a valley which stretched from south to north. Here we passed the night under a splendid mulberry tree, which could cover with its shade a hundred men.

Farther on we reached another city, and saw on the road a well more than a hundred feet deep, where an old man, a Mohammedan, had a bullock which turned the draw-beam and raised water for thirsty people. The emperor Chinghiz, when passing here, had seen this man, and ordered that he should be exempted from taxes and duties.

On the 18th of the eleventh month (December 3), after crossing a great river, we arrived at the northern side of the great city of Sie-mi-sz'-kan. We were met in the suburb by the T'ai shi [the highest Chinese minister; the emperor's counselor] Yi-la kuo kung, the chief officers of the Mongol army, the chiefs of the Mohammedans, &c. and having pitched a great number of tents, we rested there.

Chung lu (the adjutant), who had left the master, and hastened to inform the emperor, was found detained here by some hindrances on the road. He said to the master: "On our road, at a distance of about a thousand li, is a great river (the Amu river). I have been informed that the rebels have destroyed the floating bridge and the boats there. Besides this, we are now in the depth of winter. I think it would be better to wait and start in spring." The master agreed, and some time afterwards we entered the city (of Samarkand) by the north-eastern gate.

Samarkand is laid out on the borders of canals. As it never rains in summer and autumn, the people have conducted two rivers to the city, and distributed the water through all the streets, so that every house can make use of it. Before the dynasty of the suan-tuan (Sultan of Khorezm) was overthrown, the city of Samarkand had a population of more than a hundred thousand families, but after the occupation only the fourth part remained behind. Most of the fields and gardens belong to the Mohammedans, but they are not allowed to dispose of them. They are obliged to manage their properties in conjunction with Ti-tan (i.e., Karakhitai), Chinese, and men from Ho si [Tanguts]. Chinese workmen are living everywhere. In the middle of the city there is an elevated place, about a hundred feet high, on which the new palace of the Sultan was built. Formerly the T'ai shi lived here, but as this part of the city had become insecure owing to numerous robbers, he had withdrawn to the northern side of the river. The master with his disciples then occupied the palace, declaring that Taoists have no fear. The T'ai shi furnished everything for the master's subsistence, and from day to day his veneration for him increased. We saw there peacocks and great elephants, which had come from Yin-du (India), a country situated several thousand li to the south-east.

The master remained for the winter in Samarkand, and the adjutant with several hundred soldiers proceeded to explore the road in advance. We had often visits of Chinese, who came to bow before the master. There was also an astronomer, whom the master asked about the eclipse, which had happened on the 1st of the fifth month. The astronomer said: "At this place (Samarkand), between seven and nine o'clock in the morning it was at its greatest, when six-tenths of the sun were eclipsed."

The master then remarked that he observed the same eclipse on the river Lu ku, and just at noon it was total; but that when he arrived in his journey to the south-west at the Kin shan (Altai mountains), the people told him that at that place the eclipse was at its greatest at ten o'clock in the morning, and seven-tenths of the sun were eclipsed. Thus the same eclipse was seen at different places in different aspects.

Kuny Ying ta, in his commentary on the Ch' un ts'iu (Spring and Autumn Annals by Confucius), says: "When it happens that the moon stands opposite the sun, we have an eclipse; but it is only observable for those who are straight under the moon. As regards those who are distant from this spot, the aspect of the eclipse changes for them at every thousand li. If one take, for instance, a fan, and put it before a light, then a place will be seen entirely covered by the shadow; whereas on the sides, where there is gradually more light, one is by degrees farther removed from the overshadowed place."

At the end of the twelfth intercalary month (beginning of February), 1222, the adjutant returned from his exploration, and said to the master: "The second prince has moved out with his army, and the bridges have been repaired. I had sent to his encampment to inform him that the master intended to present himself to the emperor. The prince said that the emperor was then staying southeast of the Ta süe shan but that the road by which the master would be obliged to pass was covered with deep snow to an extent of about a hundred li. Therefore the prince invited the master to come to his encampment, and wait there for the favourable time for starting. The prince offered also to give the master a convoy of Mongol soldiers." After Chung lu had finished his report, the master replied (declining the offer): "I have heard that the country south of the (Amu) river is completely destitute of vegetable aliments; and I use only rice, meal, and vegetables. Please express my excuse to the prince."

In the first month (February and March), 1222, the ba-lan (trees) began to flower. The ba-lan (fruit) resembles small peaches, the fruit being gathered and eaten in autumn. The taste is like that of the hu t'ao (walnut).

On the 2d of the second month (March 15), the time of the equinox, the blossoms of the peach trees dropped.

The astronomer Pang Li Kung and others invited the master to walk outside the city to the west. The adjutant and some officers accompanied us, and brought wine with them. The day was fine and the air delicious, the flowers and the trees were in their full freshness; everywhere we saw lakes, orchards, terraces, towers, and tents. We lay down on the grass, and were all very happy together, talking about matters sublime.

The 15th of the second month (March 28) was a holiday (in honour of Lao tsz', the founder of the Tao sect). The officers begged the master again to take a walk with them west of the city. There were gardens and groves succeeding one another uninterruptedly to an extent of more than a hundred li. Even Chinese gardens cannot be compared (with those of Samarkand), but the gardens in that country are very quiet; no singing of birds is heard there.

At the beginning of the 3d month (middle of April) A-li-sien arrived from the Emperor's encampment with the following decree: "Sainted man, thou hast arrived from the country where the sun rises; thou hast met with great difficulties in crossing mountains and plains; indeed, thou hast taken great pains. I am now about to return, but I wait impatiently for thine explanation to me of the doctrine of the Tao. Do not delay meeting me." The adjutant, Chung lu, received an imperial order: "Invite him to come. If you accomplish my wishes I shall reward you." The Emperor also gave an order to Chenhai: "Accompany and protect the master on his way; then you will experience my benevolence." Besides this, the wan hu (commander of ten thousand), Bo-lu-dji, received an order to escort the master through the Iron gate.

The master inquired of A-li-sien about the way, who reported: "I left this place (Samarkand) on the 13th of the first month (February 23), and, after three days' travelling to the south-east, passed T'ie men kuan (the Iron gate) ; five days later I crossed a great river (the Amu or Oxus). On the 1st of the second month (March 13) I passed over the high snowy mountain (Hindukush), where the snow was very deep. By pushing in my whip I could only penetrate one half of the bed, even on the trodden path the snow lay five feet deep. Thence proceeding to the south, I arrived at the encampment of the Emperor. When I informed the Emperor of your arrival, he was much rejoiced. He ordered me to rest several days and then return."

The master then set out on the 15th of the third month (April 26), leaving behind three of his disciples. He took five or six with him. Chung lu and the others accompanied him. After four days' travelling we passed the city of Kie-shi. There Bo-lu-dji, who had previously received orders, escorted the master through the T'ie men kuan with a hundred Mongol and Mohammedan soldiers. We crossed the mountains in a south-eastern direction, and found them very high.

Masses of rocks were lying scattered about. The escort themselves pulled the carts, and took two days to pass the other side of the mountains. We proceeded along a river to the south, and our soldiers entered the mountains to the north to pursue the robbers. Five days after we crossed a small river in a boat, the banks of it being covered with a dense forest. Thence in seven days we reached a large river, and crossed it in a boat; its name was A-mu mu-lien.

Proceeding to the south-east, we stopped in the evening near an ancient aqueduct, the banks of which were covered with dense groves of lu-wei. The large ones preserve their green leaves during the whole winter. We made sticks from them, and they were so strong that they did not break when we used them for supporting the shafts of the carts during the night. On the smaller ones the leaves wither and are renewed in spring. More to the south, in the mountains, there is a large kind of bamboo with a pith, which the soldiers use for spears. We saw, also, lizards three feet in length and of a dark colour. We were now at the 29th of the third month (May 10), and six days later, the 5th of the fourth month (May 16), we arrived at the encampment of the Emperor, who had sent one of his high officers to meet the master. After being installed in his lodging, the master presented himself to the Emperor, who greeted him, and said: "You were invited by the other courts (the Kin and the Sung), but you refused. Now you have come to see me, having traversed a road of ten thousand li.

I am much gratified." The master answered: "The wild man of the mountains came to see the emperor by order of your majesty; it was the will of Heaven." Chinghiz invited him to sit down, and ordered a meal to be set before him. After this he asked: "Sainted man, you have come from a great distance. Have you a medicine of immortality?" The master replied: "There are means for preserving life, but no medicines for immortality." Chinghiz lauded him for his sincerity and candour. By imperial order two tents were pitched for the master east of the emperor's tents. The emperor gave him the title of shen sien (the immortal).

At the beginning of the hot season the master went with the emperor to the snowy mountains, to pass the summer there.

The 14th of the fourth month (May 25), 1222, was fixed for explaining the doctrine of the Tao (true doctrine) to the emperor; but just as the time arrived, news was received that the Mohammedan rebels in the mountains were about to renew hostilities. The emperor decided himself to attack the enemy. Therefore the day for the master's explanations was postponed until the 1st of the tenth month, which was a felicitous day. The master begged permission to return (to Samarkand), but the emperor said: "Will you not be too much fatigued to make the journey a second time?" The master replied "It is only twenty days' journey;" but the Emperor objected: "There is nobody to escort you." The master answered: "There is a man, Yang Akou, who has received orders to go with me." The emperor then assented, and after three days he gave orders that Yang Akou should take a thousand horsemen and conduct the master back by another way (than that he had come).

Proceeding on this way, we crossed a high mountain, in which is the Shi men (Stone gate), and at a distance the rocks had the appearance of candles. An immense slab lay across these rocks, like a bridge, and beneath was a rapid torrent. Many of the soldiers' donkeys were drowned in crossing this torrent, and on its borders many dead bodies were seen lying. This defile had been taken by the armies a short time before we passed.

On our way we saw men returning from the war, who carried with them a great many corals. Some of our accompanying officers bought about fifty coral trees for two yi of silver, the biggest of them more than a foot in length; but, journeying on horseback, it was impossible to carry them unbroken.

We travelled in the daytime, and profited also by the fresh nights. In five or six days (it is not said from what place) we arrived at Sie-mi-sz'-kan, or as the city is called by the Ta shi (Karakhitai), Ho chung fu (the city between the rivers). The officers came to meet the master, and directed him to his former lodging (in the new palace), which was situated on the northern side of the river. This river (the Zarafshan) has its sources in the snowy mountains (east of Samarkand), therefore its water is very cold. The palace in which the master lived was on a hill about a hundred feet in height. It was reflected in the bright water of the river. In the fifth month (June and July), during the hot season, the master was accustomed to sit at the northern window and enjoy the breeze, while at night he slept on the terrace of the roof; and in the sixth month (July-August), the hottest time of the year, he bathed in the basin. Thus the master spent his time in the far west.

The arable land in Ho chung (Samarkand) is suitable for all kinds of corn. Only the k'iao mai (buckwheat) and the to tou (soya bean) are not found there. In the fourth month (May) wheat ripens; when gathered, the people pile it up in heaps. In the sixth month the intendant of the t'ai shi made a present to the master of water-melons, which in this country are very fragrant and sweet, and of enormous size. We have no water-melons like these in China. When, in the sixth month, the second prince returned, Chung lu requested the master to give him some of his water-melons for a present to the prince. The country is very rich in fruits and vegetables, but yü (colocasia) and chestnuts are wanting. The k'ie [eggplant] there have the shape of enormous fingers, and are of a purplish colour. Men and women braid their hair. The caps of the nien at a distance resemble hills. They are adorned with embroidery and tassels. All officers wear such caps. The men of the lower classes wrap their heads about with a piece of white mo-sz', about six feet long. The women of the chieftains and the rich envelop their heads with a piece of gauze, from five to six feet long, and of a black or dark red colour. Sometimes flowers and plants or other figures are embroidered upon it. They wear their hair dishevelled. Sometimes they put wadding under it (under the covering of the head?). The women of the lower classes do not braid their hair into a queue on the top of the head. They cover their heads with linen and other stuff, and thus bear some resemblance to our (Buddhist) nuns. As to their dress, men as well as women are wont to put on a kind of shirt made of woollen stuff, of a white colour, which has the appearance of a bag, narrow in the upper part, wide beneath, with sleeves attached to it. If a man grows poor, his wife takes another husband. In the case of the husband going on a journey and not returning home within the space of three months, his wife is allowed to marry another husband. But there is one thing very odd among these people. Some of their women have beards and moustaches.

The carts, boats, and implements of husbandry in that country are very different in appearance from those used in China. Their weapons are made of steel. Most of the vessels they use are made of copper, but there are also found vessels of porcelain, as in China. The vessels for wine are made only of glass. The money they use in commerce is of gold, but has no hole. On both sides are Mohammedan letters.

The people are very strong and tall. They sometimes bear very heavy burdens on their backs without any crossbeam. There are men well versed in books, and who are exclusively taken up with writing. They are called Da-shi-ma. In winter they fast for a whole month, during which every day, at night, the superior kills a sheep for the meal, when all sit round cross-legged, and eat the whole night till morning. Besides this, they have six fastings in other months.

They have high buildings [minarets] with rafters on the top, standing out about ten feet all around, and on these rafters an empty pavilion rises, hung with tassels. Every morning and evening the superior [muezzin] goes up and bows to the west. They call this kao t'ien (praying to heaven), for they believe not in Buddhism or Taoism. The superior above sings in a loud tone, and the men and women, hearing his voice, meet at this place and pray below. The same custom exists throughout the whole country. Whoever neglects to perform these ceremonies is executed. The superior is dressed like the others, only his head is wrapped with a piece of white mo-sz'.

In the seventh month, as the new moon had just appeared (August 8, 1222), the master sent A-li-sien with a report to the emperor, asking about the time for the explanation of the doctrine of Tao. The answer of the emperor, written on the same report, was received on the 7th of the eighth month (September).

On the 8th of the same month (September 14) we set out for the emperor's encampment. The T'ai shi accompanied the master twenty or thirty li, and returned. On the 12th (September 18) we passed the city of lie-shi (Kash). On the 13th we were joined by a convoy of 1000 men on foot and 300 on horseback, and entered the high mountains. The route we followed now went round the T'ie men kuan (Iron gate). We crossed a river with red water, and proceeded through a defile to the south-east, where there were rocks several li in height. At the foot of the mountains is a salt spring, the water of which deposits white salt after evaporation. We took a large quantity of it with us. Farther to the south-east we ascended a mountain which forms a watershed. To the west we saw a high valley, which seemed to be filled up with ice, but it was salt. On the top of the mountain there was a red-coloured salt, with the appearance of stone, which the master tasted himself. In the eastern countries (China, Mongolia) salt is only found in low grounds, but here it is also met with in the mountains. The Mohammedans eat cakes with salt. When thirsty they drink water, even in winter. Poor men sell water in jars.

On the 14th of the eighth month (September 20) we arrived at the south-western foot of the Iron gate. Here the issue of the defile is bordered by terrible rocks. One on the left has fallen down, and the river to an extent of a li was covered by rocks.

On the 15th (September 21) we arrived at the river (the Amu river again). It resembles the Yellow River in China, and runs in a north-western direction. Having crossed it in a boat, we stopped on the southern bank. To the west there is a mountain fortress called T'uan ba- la, which is a strong position. On our road we met Chen-kun, the physician of the third prince (Ogotai). We proceeded up the stream (in a boat); but after thirty li the water was too shallow, when (we went on shore, and) travelling during the night, we passed Ban- li [Balkh], a very large city, the inhabitants of which had revolted not long ago, and fled. We heard the barking of the dogs in the city. At daybreak, after taking breakfast, we went to the east more than twenty li to a river running northward, which could be forded on horseback, and passed the night on the eastern bank of this river.

On the 22nd of the eighth month (September 28) Chenhai came to meet the master, and accompanied him to the emperor's encampment. On his arrival Chen-hai asked the master whether lie wished to be introduced immediately to the emperor, or to rest first. The master begged to be presented. It must be said here that the professors of the Tao (true doctrine), when admitted to an audience, were never required to fall upon their knees or to bow their heads to the ground. On entering the imperial tent, they only made a bow and placed the hands together (a sign of esteem among Chinese monks).

The master was then presented to the emperor, who ordered tung to [kumis] to be set before him; but the master firmly refused to drink it. The emperor asked him how lie was supplied with victuals in the city where he lived (Samarkand); when [sic: then?] the master expressed his satisfaction. Next day the emperor sent a man to invite the sage to dine every day with his majesty. The master replied: "I am a wild man of the mountains,; I cultivate the true doctrine (Tao), and therefore I like seclusion." The emperor then permitted him to live as he liked.

On the 27th of the eighth month (October 3) the emperor set out on his return to the north (and the master accompanied him). The emperor on the road often sent wine made from grapes, water-melons, and other eatables to the master.

On the 1st of the ninth month (October 6), 1222, we crossed the river (Amu) on a floating bridge, and proceeded to the north.

On the 15th (October 20), at the suggestion of the master, Chinghiz ordered a tent to be prepared for the explanation of the Taoist doctrine. Chen-hai and Chung lu were present at the explanation. The T'ai shi (councillor) A-hai translated the words of the master into Mongol for the emperor. The emperor was highly edified, and the discourse of the sage pleased his heart. On the 19th (October 24) the night was bright, and the emperor called the master again to continue his explanations, with which he was much satisfied. On the 23rd the master was again invited. The emperor ordered his words to be written down in Chinese as well as in Mongol.

After this we followed the emperor in his march to the east (i.e., back to Mongolia), and approaching the great city of Sie-mi-sz'-kan (Samarkand), encamped twenty li west of it. On the first of the l0th month (November 5) the master solicited permission to visit the place where he lived before (the palace on the hill near Samarkand), which the emperor granted. The imperial camp then was thirty li east of Samarkand. On the 6th the master appeared again before the emperor, together with the councilor A-hai (who was the interpreter). Chinghiz asked the master: "Shall the bystanders withdraw?" to which he replied that they might remain, and explained to the emperor as follows:

"The wild man of the mountains these many years has devoted himself to the investigation of Tao, and likes to be in solitude. Around the tent of your majesty I hear the noise of your soldiers, and I cannot keep my mind quiet ; therefore I solicit from your majesty the permission to travel henceforth alone, in advance or behind. This will be a great favour to the wild man of the mountains." The emperor assented.

At that time (November) rain first began to fall, and the grass became green again. In that country, in the middle of the eleventh month (December), rain and snow became more frequent and moistened the ground. The master went to Samarkand and distributed the remainder of his provisions to the hungry people, who were very numerous.

On the 26th of the eleventh month (December 29), 1222, we set out on our journey. On the 23rd of the 12th month (January 25, 1223) there was a snowfall, and such all intense cold that a great number of our bullocks and horses died on the road. Proceeding to the east, we crossed three days later (January 28) the Ho-ch'an mulien (Syr-daria), and reached the encampment of the emperor (who was also on his homeward journey). We were told there that during the past night the bridge across the river had been broken down and carried away.

([Bretschneider:] Chinghiz again had discourses with the sage, but I omit them as being of no interest.)

On the 1st of the first month (Chinese new year, February 2, 1223) the master took leave. The commander-in-chief, the physician-in-ordinary, and the diviner-in-chief came to congratulate the master.

On the 11th (February 12) we proceeded again eastward. Sie-mi-sz'-kan was now behind us, at a distance of more than a thousand li. On the 21st (February 22) we went to the east of one station, and arrived at a broad valley (plain) well watered and rich in grass, where we stayed for some time, in order to restore our tired horses and bullocks. Sai-lan (Sairam) is three days' journey from this place to the north-east.

On the 7th of the second month (March 9) the master was admitted to an audience and said to the emperor: "At the time the wild man of the mountains left the seashore (Shan tung), he gave his word to be back again in three years. It is indeed my ardent desire to see my native mountains again in this third year." The emperor replied "I am myself returning to the east. Will not you go with me? " Then the master said: "I have explained all your majesty wished to hear; I have nothing more to say. It would be better for me to go in advance." He solicited earnestly to be sent home; but the emperor refused his assent, saying: "Wait a little; in three or five days my sons will arrive; there are still some points in your doctrine not quite clear to my mind. Having understood all, I will not object to your going home."

On the 8th the emperor was hunting in the mountains to the east, and in shooting a boar he was thrown from his horse. The wounded boar stopped, and the emperor was in danger.

([Bretschneider:] I omit Ch' ang ch'un's conversation with Chinghiz about the necessity of desisting from the pleasure of hunting at his advanced age.)

On the 24th of the second month the master ventured again to solicit his being sent home ; but the emperor said: "Wait a little. I must think over the presents to give you on your departure;" so he was again obliged to remain. But on the 7th of the third month (April 8) he renewed his request, when the emperor made him a present of bullocks and horses. The master refused, saying that post-horses would be sufficient for him; and the emperor granted a decree, with the imperial seal, which released all professors of the doctrine of Tao from taxes. He ordered A-li-sien to accompany the master on his journey to the east, appointing him süan ch'ai (imperial envoy). Meng-gu-dai and Go-la-ba-hai were appointed his assistants.

On the 10th of the third month (April 11), 1223, the master finally took leave of the emperor, and we started; all the officers, from the ta-la-han down to the lower ranks, accompanied the master more than twenty li, carrying with them wine and rare fruits, and all were moved to tears.

In three days we arrived at Sai-lan (Sairam). In the mountains south of the city there are two-headed snakes, two feet long, which are frequently seen by the natives.

On the 15th (April 16) the disciples of the master went out of the city to sacrifice at the tomb of the disciple who died there (on the journey hither). We spoke about carrying with us his mortal remains, but the master said "The body, formed temporally of the four elements, decays without any value; but the soul has a real existence, is free, and cannot be grasped." Then we spoke no more about that, and the next day we started again (April 17).

On the 23rd of the third month (April 24) we were joined by the imperial envoy A-gou (who had received orders) to accompany the master on his journey-along the southern bank of the Ch'ui mu-lien. Ten days later we were at a distance of more than a hundred li west of A li ma (Almalik), and crossed a large river. On the 5th of the fourth month (May 5), having arrived at a Garden east of the city of A li ma, Chang kung, the architect-in-chief of the second prince, requested the master to cross the river for the purpose of inaugurating some temples on the other side ; but this excursion was not brought about. ([Bretschneider:] I omit the details.)

In the evening (of the day they started from A li ma) we arrived at the foot of the Yin shan,spent the night there, and the next day passed again the forty-eight bridges, and proceeded fifty li up the torrent to the Heavenly lake.

Thence we went in a north-eastern direction, crossed the Yin shan (i.e., a branch of it), and after two days' journey, came to the same post-road which we had followed on our journey hither, and which leads south of the Kin shan (Altai) to a great river. Then proceeding from south to north, we passed to the eastern side of the Kin shan.

On the 28th of the fourth month (May 28) there was a great snowfall, and the next day all the mountains around were white. We then went in a north-eastern direction along mountains, and in three days reached the front-side of the A-bu-han mountain. The disciples (left by Ch'ang ch'un here in a new-built monastery) and the others came a long distance to meet the master, and directed him to the monastery Si hia kuan. Just as the master got out of his cart it began to rain, when all were very glad and congratulated each other, saying: "In this country it very seldom rains in summer; rain and thunder rarely happen except in the mountains to the south and to the north; but this summer rain is abundant. For the present fall we are indebted to the sanctity of the master."

The people of this country in ordinary years irrigate their fields and gardens by means of aqueducts. In the eighth month (September) wheat ripens, and there is then no rain. At the time the corn ripens it is damaged by mice (or rats); these mice are all white. In this country cold predominates, and the fruits ripen late in the year. In the fifth month (June) we found on the borders of the river, at a depth of about one foot, ice in the ground about a foot thick; and the master sent his servants every day after dinner to bring some. To the south a high mountain range is to be seen, covered with masses of snow, which never melts even in the hottest season of the year.

There are many remarkable things in this country. A little to the west of this place, on the border of a lake, there is a "wind-hill," the top of which consists of white clay cracked in many places. In the second and third months (March, April) the wind rises here and howls in the rocks and cavities of the southern mountains. This is only the beginning; when the wind first comes out from the wind-hill, numerous whirls are seen like ram's horns; but after some time these whirls unite to form a hurricane, which raises sand, throws stones, lifts off roofs, and uproots trees. In the river to the south-east there are three or four watermills; but when the water reaches the plain, it becomes scanty, and finally disappears. In the mountains are coals. To the east there are two springs, which in wintertime increase like rivers or lakes ; the water then is absorbed by the ground, but suddenly it appears again, carrying fish and shrimps along with it. Often the water overflows the houses, but in spring it gradually disappears?

To the north-west of this country, at a distance of about a thousand li and more, there is a country called Kien-Kien-chow, where good iron is found, and where squirrels abound and wheat is cultivated. A great number of Chinese live there, and carry on the business of manufacturing different kinds of silk and other stuffs.

From the monastery (of Si hia kuan) the Kin shan (Altai) is visible, where much hail falls (see note 130). In the fifth and sixth months there is more than ten feet of snow. On the northern slopes of the Kin shan there are pines about a hundred feet high.

The land is interspersed with deserts. In this country the jou ts'ung jung grows. The natives (Mongols) call this plant so-yen. In their language water is called wu-su, and grass ai-bu-su.

The assembled people said to the master: "This country here is in a state of deep barbarism. From the most remote time the people have never heard of the true doctrine. We had only to do with the charms of mountain goblins and other bad spirits; but ever since the master founded a monastery here, there has been a service established. On the first and the fifteenth of every month the people have assembled and have taken a vow not to kill living creatures. Certainly that was an effect of the true doctrine (Tao); what else could have produced this change? At first the Taoists here had much to complain of the malice of bad men, and were not left quiet. There was the physician Lo sheng, who always tried to annoy the Taoists and to injure them. But once passing by the Taoist temple, he was thrown from his horse and broke his leg. Then he was moved to repentance, owned that he was punished for his sins, and begged pardon."

A-li-sien and the others said to the master: "The southern route has much sand and is very stony; little grass and water are found there. Our traveling company is numerous; the horses will be extremely fatigued, and we have to fear many delays on the road." The master replied : "Then it would be better to start in three parties."

On the 7th of the fifth month (June 6), 1223, he sent six of his disciples in advance, and started himself with six disciples on the 14th (June 13). He was accompanied for twenty li, by the most respectable people of the place; then they got down from their horses, bowed before the master and shed tears. The master spurred on his horse and departed quickly. On the 18th the remaining five disciples set out.

Proceeding eastward, on the 16th (June 15) the master crossed a high mountain, which was covered with snow. It was very cold. The post-horses were changed near the tent.

On the 17th the master did not eat anything; he only drank rice-water from time to time. Proceeding to the south-east, we crossed a great sandy plain, where we found grass and trees infested with mosquitos. We passed the night on the eastern bank of a river. Farther on the master travelled from time to time in his cart. The disciples asked him from what complaint he suffered; to which he replied: "My malady cannot be understood by physicians; it is a purification by the help of the sainted men and the sages. I cannot get well suddenly; but you need not be anxious." The disciples were afflicted, and did not understand his words. Then one of them had a dream, in which a spirit said to him: "Be not alarmed about the master's sickness. After his arrival in China he will get well again." We proceeded by a sandy road for more than 300 li; water and grass were very scarce. We travelled uninterruptedly; even at night our horses did not rest. Finally, after two days we emerged from the sand, and were then near the northern frontier of the Hia (Tangut empire). Here huts and tents became more frequent, and we had less difficulty in getting horses. The disciples who travelled behind reached us here.

On the 21st of the sixth month (July 19), 1223, we stopped at Yü yang kuan. The master still continued to abstain from food. Next day we passed the customs barrier and reached fifty li to the east of it, Feng chou, where the first officers of the place came to meet the master, who began again to eat as he was accustomed to do.

We were then at the end of the summer, and the master was in the habit of sitting at the northern window of the house in which he stayed. At the request of the master of the house he wrote some verses on silk paper.

On the 1st of the seventh month (July 29) we started again, and arrived after three days at Hia shui. The next day we left, and on the 9th (August 6) arrived at Yün chung, where the master spent more than twenty days. The military commandant of Süan te sent an express to Yün chung with a letter to the master and an offer of cart and horses.

At the beginning of the eighth month (end of August) the master started, and proceeding eastward, we reached Yang hö, passed Po teng, T'ien ch'eng, Huai an, and crossed the river Hun ho. The commandant met the master far out of the city (of Süan te), and lodged him at the monastery Chao yuan kuan. The Taoists received the master with great distinction, and told him that in the last winter some of them saw Ch'ao kung (the disciple who died at Sairaui) entering the monastery and leading a horse by the bridle. All came to meet him, but he disappeared suddenly. He was also seen at other places.

The princes, dignitaries, commanders, and other officers in Northern China addressed letters to the master inviting him to visit them. These invitations succeeded each other like the spokes of a rolling wheel; but the master answered that he was sorry he could not divide himself into several bodies, to satisfy the wishes of all.

According to a vow taken at the time Ch'ang ch'un passed the battlefield of Ye-hu ling, covered with white human bones, there was on the 15th (September 10) a service performed by Ch'ang ch'un's disciples in Te hing, at the monastery of Lung yang kuan, to help the destitute souls to pass over. After the service, an officer from the emperor (Chinghiz) arrived to inquire about the master's journey, health, &c. Ch'ang ch'un spent the winter in Lung yang kuan.

The governor of Yen king (now Peking) and other officers from that city sent an express with a letter to the master, in order to invite him to stay in the monastery of Ta t'ien chang kuan, to which he assented. At Nan kou, in the monastery of Shen yu kuan, the Taoists of Yen king met him. The next day venerable old men, men and women, assembled from all sides, and accompanied the master with fragrant flowers when he entered Yen king, and the people bowing before him obstructed the road.

At the time the master started for the west, the friends wished to know when he would return, to which he replied: "In three years--in three years;" and indeed his prophecy was realised, for it was on the 7th of the first month (January 28), 1224, he arrived at the monastery of Ch'ang tien kuan.

[(Bretschneider:) Having brought back the venerable traveller from a long and painful journey to his native soil, I break off the narrative of his adventures. The Si yu ki continues Ch'ang ch'un's biography until his death ; but the further events of his life are of little interest, and have nothing to do with my programme. I will only briefly state that the master remained at Peking. By order of Chinghiz, the ground of the gardens of the northern palace of the Kin was given to him for the purpose of establishing there a Taoist monastery. This monastery was built on the S'iung hua island, and the people were forbidden to gather fuel in the park of the island and to fish in the lake. The master, who lived there, sometimes took a walk to the top of the hill on the island, and enjoyed the magnificent view he had of the surrounding Gardens. Farther on in the narrative we read: "On the 23rd of the sixth month (July 8), 1227, it was reported to the master that, owing to heavy rain, the southern embankment of the lake had fallen down, and that the water had crushed into the eastern lake, so that it was heard at a distance of several li. After this all fish and tortoises disappeared, and the lake became dry." Ch'ang ch'un took this for an omen of his death, and indeed he died on the 9th of the seventh month (July 23), 1227.

Next year his disciples, with the help of a great number of other Taoists, who had arrived from different parts of China, built for the mortal remains of the sage a monastery, the buildings of which were finished in forty days. The 9th of the seventh month (August to), 1228, was fixed for the ceremony of transferring and burying the body. During the sixth month (July) heavy rain fell uninterruptedly. The people were afraid that the ceremony would be hindered; but on the 1st of the seventh month (August 2) the heavens suddenly cleared up, and all were much gratified. When the coffin was opened, the appearance of the master was the same as he had showed in his life. During three days people came from far and near, princes, officers, and others, more than ten thousand. All were astonished at this wonder and laid their hands on their foreheads. The funeral ceremonies continued three days.

On the 8th of the seventh month (August 9), at eight o'clock in the morning, at first black cranes flew past from the south-west, then followed white cranes 278 The people looked at them with astonishment. On the 9th at midnight was the last funeral service, after which the mortal remains (literally, the exuviae of the immortal part of man) of the master were buried in the monastery. This monastery received the name Po yün kuan (the Monastery of the White Clouds.)]

www.ingramcontent.com/pod-product-compliance
Lightning Source LLC
LaVergne TN
LVHW010943110826
845149LV00013B/2733

* 9 7 8 1 9 5 7 9 9 0 4 4 6 *